Ramadan

Katie Gillespie

AV² provides enriched content that supplements and complements this book. Weigl's AV² books strive to create inspired learning and engage young minds in a total learning experience.

Your AV² Media Enhanced books come alive with...

Audio
Listen to sections of the book read aloud.

Key Words
Study vocabulary, and complete a matching word activity.

Go to www.av2books.com, and enter this book's unique code.

BOOK CODE

J925677

Video
Watch informative video clips.

Quizzes
Test your knowledge.

Embedded Weblinks
Gain additional information for research.

Slide Show
View images and captions, and prepare a presentation.

AV² by Weigl brings you media enhanced books that support active learning.

Try This!
Complete activities and hands-on experiments.

... and much, much more!

Published by AV² by Weigl
350 5th Avenue, 59th Floor New York, NY 10118
Website: www.av2books.com

Library of Congress Control Number: 2015934750

ISBN 978-1-4896-3633-1 (hardcover)
ISBN 978-1-4896-3634-8 (softcover)
ISBN 978-1-4896-3635-5 (single user eBook)
ISBN 978-1-4896-3636-2 (multi-user eBook)

Printed in the United States of America in Brainerd, Minnesota
1 2 3 4 5 6 7 8 9 0 19 18 17 16 15

072015
070715

Editor: Katie Gillespie   Design and Layout: Ana María Vidal

Every reasonable effort has been made to trace ownership and to obtain permission to reprint copyright material. The publisher would be pleased to have any errors or omissions brought to its attention so that they may be corrected in subsequent printings.

Weigl acknowledges Getty Images, iStock, Corbis, and Alamy as the primary image suppliers for this title.

Let's Celebrate American Holidays
Ramadan

CONTENTS

4

Ramadan is celebrated during the ninth month of the Islamic calendar. It is a time for Muslims to show their dedication to Allah.

Allah is the name of the god that Muslims worship.

Ramadan is an important holiday for people of the Islamic faith. It has been celebrated for about 1,400 years.

7

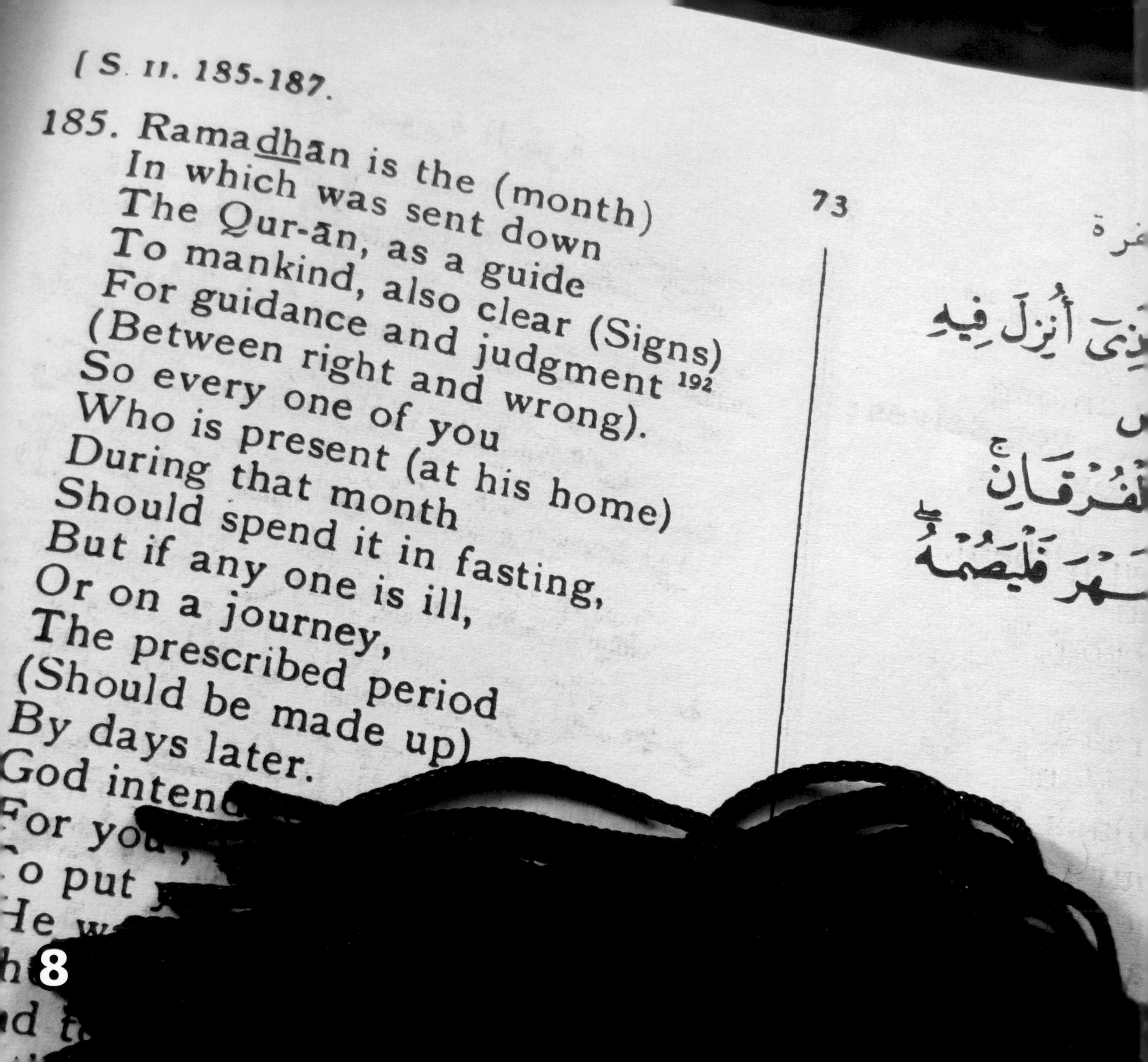

185. Ramadhan is the (month)
In which was sent down
The Qur-an, as a guide
To mankind, also clear (Signs)
For guidance and judgment [192]
(Between right and wrong).
So every one of you
Who is present (at his home)
During that month
Should spend it in fasting,
But if any one is ill,
Or on a journey,
The prescribed period
(Should be made up)
By days later.
God inten...
For you...
To put...
He w...
...d t...

73

زة

ئِذِى أُنزِلَ فِيهِ

لَفُرْقَانِ ج

هَرَ فَلْيَصُمْهُ

The Islamic religion is based on five rules. They are called the five Pillars of Islam.

People go to places of worship to pray during Ramadan. A Muslim place of worship is called a mosque.

The holiest mosque in the Islamic faith is the Great Mosque in Mecca, Saudi Arabia.

Millions of people come together each year to celebrate Ramadan. Special activities are held all over America.

The first White House Ramadan celebration was hosted by Thomas Jefferson in 1805.

Many Muslims fast during Ramadan. This means they do not eat or drink between sunrise and sunset.

Fasting helps people feel closer to Allah.

15

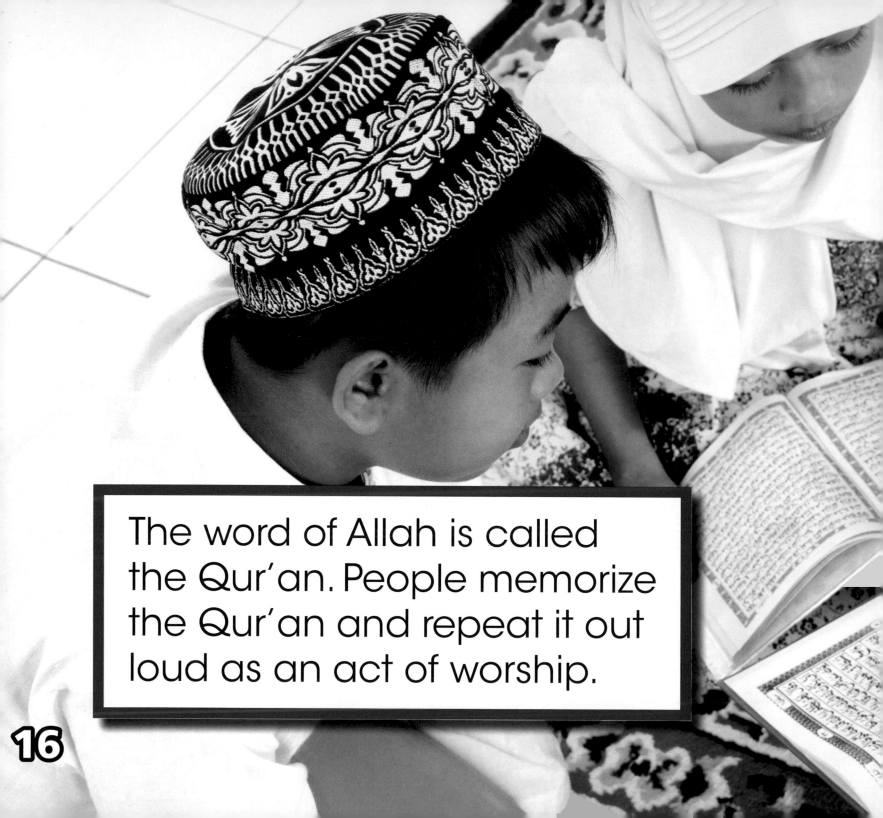

The word of Allah is called the Qur'an. People memorize the Qur'an and repeat it out loud as an act of worship.

The Qur'an was passed on by Allah to a man named Muhammad.

17

Helping others is part of the Islamic religion. Giving to charity is especially important during Ramadan.

19

The end of Ramadan is celebrated with a special festival called Eid al-Fitr. This means the "festival of the fast breaking."

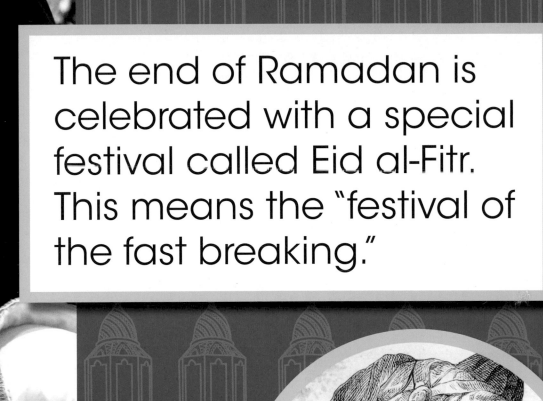

Muhammad celebrated the first Eid al-Fitr in AD 624.

RAMADAN FACTS

These pages provide more detail about the interesting facts found in the book. They are intended to be used by adults as a learning support to help young readers round out their knowledge of each holiday featured in the *Let's Celebrate American Holidays* series.

Pages 4–5

Ramadan is celebrated during the ninth month of the Islamic calendar. This calendar has 12 months, totaling about 354 days. It is based on the cycles of the Moon. The start and end of the holiday are based on the appearance of a new moon. This is why the dates of Ramadan vary from year to year. Although Ramadan is not a federal holiday in the United States, many Islamic businesses and organizations have special hours of operation to accommodate prayer times.

Pages 6–7

Ramadan is an important holiday for people of the Islamic faith. It is a time for self-reflection, group prayer, and recitation of the holy scripture called the Qur'an. Muslims believe that those who fast and pray during the month of Ramadan will have their past sins forgiven by Allah. Bad behavior is always considered wrong, but it is disapproved of even more during Ramadan. This holiday is a good opportunity for Muslims to demonstrate their religious devotion.

Pages 8–9

The Islamic religion is based on five rules. The five Pillars of Islam are shahada, salat, zakat, sawm, and hajj. Shahada declares that "There is no God but Allah and Muhammad is His prophet." Salat refers to Islamic prayer. Muslims must pray in the early morning, at noon, mid-afternoon, at sunset, and in the evening every day. Zakat requires Muslims to make regular donations to charity. Sawm refers to fasting during Ramadan. Hajj says that all Muslims must visit the holy city of Mecca.

Pages 10–11

People go to places of worship to pray during Ramadan. Many people attend mosques around the United States. They get together to give thanks and praise to Allah. Muslims are also expected to make at least one trip to Mecca during their lives. Called a pilgrimage, this journey is the fifth rule, or Pillar of Islam. Millions of people make the pilgrimage to the Great Mosque in Mecca every year. It is the site of the holiest shrine in Islam, called the Ka'bah.

Pages 12–13

Millions of people come together each year to celebrate Ramadan. Events are held around the world, including several American cities. They are organized to show the American Muslim community's dedication to Allah. For instance, an annual event called Eid Festival is held in Anaheim, to unite residents of communities around Southern California. Other celebrations include fireworks, television specials, and popular music.

Pages 14–15

Many Muslims fast during Ramadan. During Ramadan, times of fasting depend on the Sun. People are allowed to eat and drink before the Sun rises and after it sets, but must fast during the day. Not all Muslims participate in this activity. People who are sick or traveling long distances are not expected to fast. Children younger than 12 and pregnant women are not required to fast either.

Pages 16–17

The word of Allah is called the Qur'an. It tells of Allah and creation. The Qur'an also teaches values, such as how to live a good life. Muslims believe that a man named Muhammad was the last Islamic prophet, or religious teacher, inspired by Allah. The words of Allah were revealed to Muhammad on the 27th night of Ramadan, known today as the Night of Power. Muhammad passed these words on to be written down as the Qur'an.

Pages 18–19

Helping others is part of the Islamic religion. Charity is important all year, but it is even more so during Ramadan. People participate in charitable events around the world. Donations are sometimes given before the Eid prayer occurs. In some places, meals are served to those in need. One popular organization is LIFE's Ramadan Food Basket. Located in Southfield, Michigan, it offers food to families in need during Ramadan.

Pages 20–21

The end of Ramadan is celebrated with a special festival called Eid al-Fitr. It begins once the new moon has been seen. People get together to celebrate and enjoy large meals. Street festivals are held in Muslim communities across America. They often feature carnival rides, balloons, and cotton candy. One of the largest events is at the Los Angeles Convention Center. Thousands of people come to pray and celebrate.

KEY WORDS

Research has shown that as much as 65 percent of all written material published in English is made up of 300 words. These 300 words cannot be taught using pictures or learned by sounding them out. They must be recognized by sight. This book contains 53 common sight words to help young readers improve their reading fluency and comprehension. This book also teaches young readers several important content words, such as proper nouns. These words are paired with pictures to aid in learning and improve understanding.

Page	Sight Words First Appearance
5	a, for, is, it, name, of, show, that, the, their, time, to
6	about, an, been, has, important, people, years
9	are, on, they
10	go, in, places
13	all, America, by, come, each, first, over, together, was
14	and, between, closer, do, eat, helps, many, means, not, or, this
16	as, out, word
17	man
18	others, part
21	end, with

Page	Content Words First Appearance
5	Allah, calendar, god, dedication, month, Muslims, Ramadan
6	faith, holiday
9	Pillars of Islam, religion, rules
10	Great Mosque, Mecca, Saudi Arabia, mosque, pray
13	activities, celebration, Thomas Jefferson
14	Muslims, sunrise, sunset
16	act, Qur'an
17	Muhammad
18	charity, religion
21	Eid al-Fitr, festival